# THE
# MAJOR
# COUPONING
# REFERENCE
# GUIDE

## POCKET EDITION

## MASTERING THE MARKETS

# DEDICATION

To those who want to coupon,
But don't have enough time.

You too can save money,
And time!

```
Douore coupons
HNST TEA WHT PCH      MCP      -0.50 F
  Double Coupons               -0.50 F
HNST TEA WHT PCH      MCP      -0.50 F
  Double Coupons               -0.50 F
HONEST TEA           MCP       -0.50 F
  Double Coupons               -0.50 F
HONEST TEA           MCP       -0.50 F
  Double Coupons               -0.50 F
HONEST TEA           MCP       -0.50 F
  Double Coupons               -0.50 F

     Total before savings $234.50
     Your Total Savings    $216.49
     Total after savings    $18.01
     Tax paid                $2.70
     Total                  $20.71
     Cash Tnd               $21.00
     Change                  $0.29

  Total number of items sold = 94


  YOUR  SAVINGS  SUMMARY
  BonusCard Savings          $65.99
  Double Coupons         64  $24.95
  Manufacturer's Coupons 79  $125.55
  Your Total Savings         $216.49
```

# CONTENTS

# ACKNOWLEDGMENTS

This booklet is a pocket edition to
The Major Couponing Reference Guide
The MCRG is a couponers annual guide to everything related
to couponing.  This book is updated yearly and released
every January with the latest information, store polices,
couponing websites, tricks and tidbits for all
coupon enthusiast.
This Pocket edition will provide the quick and easy reference for
those who want to get their feet wet, want to save money, but
don't have the time to go to extreme yet.

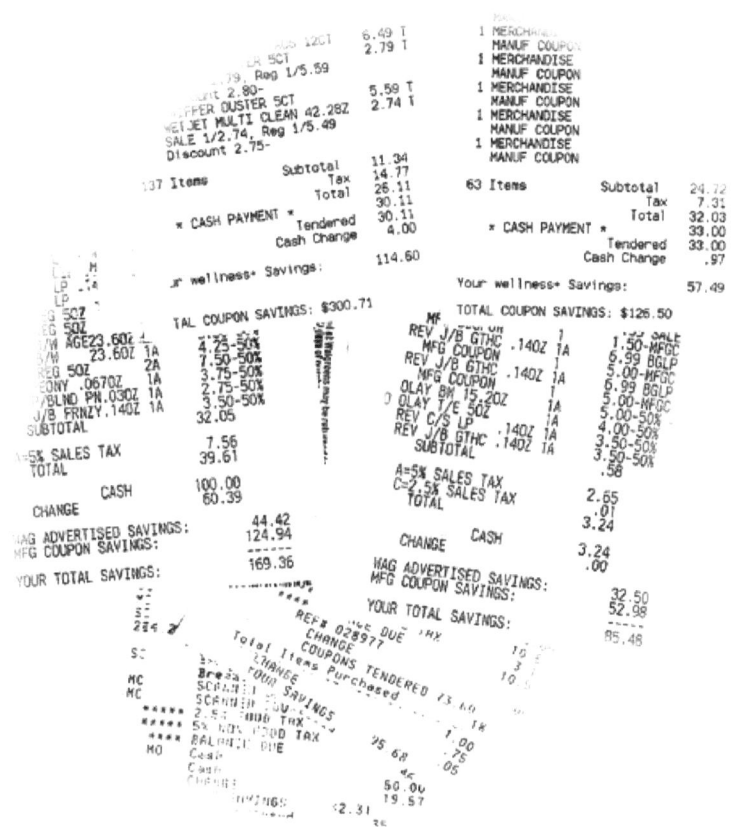

# MASTERING THE MARKET

# WHY COUPON?

Simply, to save money. Money is a negative in the grocery store, and coupons are a positive. Money you spend and coupons you save. And you can save a lot of money if you start shopping strategically. You will save on the things you already are buying. Why pay full price? You are going to buy it anyway, why not save a couple dollars in the process?

This is your reference guide that will explain every detail about couponing you could ever imagine. The Basic plan only requires 1 hour a week, and you shop like you normally do. As you save more and more money, I guarantee you will find the extra time. There are extreme couponers who spend hours and hours weekly, trust me they have learned the trrade. Some say time is money, so why not spend some time, saving your money?

There are a lot of Money Makers (coupons where the value exceeds the product). These MM will put money in your pocket and make your basket total cheaper.

It is important to read the coupon and search for the lowest price item. If a coupon is $10 for a rechargeable toothbrush and you find it at Wal-Mart for 5.67 you just made 4.33, if you order that coupon and purchase ten, you just made 43.30. This coupled with understanding the UPC of the coupon is how Extreme Couponers a mass such large shopping hauls. Every month there will be MM's and price matching sites (listed in the appendix) will help you.

Couponing is win-win, but you have to understand how they work. This is not a novel, or funny read. This is your quick guide to understanding coupons, and the best sites to further your couponitis☺

# COUPON 101

## WHAT IS A COUPON?

A manufacturer's coupon is a piece of paper with a discount for a specified product printed on it. Money goes out your pocket, coupons put money in. Money is a negative and coupons are a positive. The coupon can be used at most stores that carry the specified product. To receive your discount you must purchase the product and give the cashier the coupon. The cashier will scan the coupon and the coupon amount will be deducted from your purchase. You then pay for the remainder of the purchase.

## BASIC COUPON RULES

### You may use one coupon per indicated items purchased.

If you have two coupons to save $1 on one box of cereal, you can buy two boxes and use both coupons. The coupon will say "one coupon per purchase." If you purchase two boxes then you must have two coupons. So, you can buy ten boxes with ten coupons.

### You can use two coupons on one item.

You can use one store coupon and one manufacturer coupon on one item. Some stores will allow you to use two manufacturer coupons; you must read the policies and take advantage of the stores that still allow this. This is becoming extremely rare as stores are changing this policy. However, if you find a coupon $5 off product XXX and you have a coupon that reads buy product XXX and get ZZZ for free, you may use them both together.

**Read the coupon and disregard the picture.**

Manufacturer's usually put a picture of their most expensive product on the coupon to make you think that is what you have to buy. If you actually read the terms of the coupon, it will usually say "save on ANY brand XXX product." That means you can buy even the least expensive product and still save with the coupon.

**You can use a coupon on an item that is discounted, on sale or clearance.**

Always check the clearance section of the store before you checkout.

# Major Couponing Must Know's

- **Loyalty Cards**. - If your store offers a loyalty card then make sure to have at least two. Some stores only give the sale prices to card-holders with a limit, if you have two cards you can get the rewards twice. Write a name with a marker on the back not to get confused. You will find the newer the card the more extra rewards you may get. Stores are often more generous to new card holders to suck them in.
- **Double/Triple coupons days**. - Double/triple coupons is when the store will take your 50¢ coupon and double it making it $1. This is done automatically at the register, you do not have to do anything to take part in this promotion. First, find out if your store doubles/triples coupons. If they do then find out the maximum double/triple value and how many they will double/triple.
- **Stacking coupons**. - Some stores will allow you to use one store coupon (the discount is provided by the store) and one manufacturer coupon (the discount is provided by the manufacturer) per item.
- **Price Matching**. - Find out if your store will price match a competitors advertised price. This means that if cereal XXX is on sale for one dollar at store YYY, you can take the ad to Walmart and at checkout tell the cashier that you would like to pricematch the cereal. Show them the ad and they will sell you the product for the advertised price. And you can still use a coupon on the item. Wal-Mart is a major chain that does this.
- **Competitor coupons**. - Some stores will accept competitor's coupons.
- **Expired coupons**. – Our Military and some stores will accept them.

- **Patience is a Virtue.** - Don't go out and use your coupon immediately. **OFTEN THE LOWEST PRICE IS NEVER IN THE SAME WEEK WHEN THE COUPON COMES OUT.** Use patience and don't be in a rush to buy it at the first advertised sale. The item will be listed week after week until it expires. Matching sales with coupons will get you a good price. Combining sales plus coupons plus another promotion (rebates, double coupons, store coupons) is getting the extreme price or free!
- **One per Purchase.** - Most coupons say "one coupon per purchase" somewhere in the fine print. Some less knowledgeable cashiers will interpret that to mean you can only use one coupon per transaction/day. This is incorrect and do not accept this. Often the manager will be happy to educate the cashier. One per purchase means that you can only use one coupon per item purchased. So if you are buying 25 items and have 25 coupons then you can use them all.
- **Limits.** - Stores will sometimes put limits on the item to draw your attention and make you think it's a great deal. If granola bars are on sale 2/$4 you might not even notice it. But if it's on sale 2/$4, limit 2! Then you will likely think it's a great deal since they had to limit it. Watch out for this. If it really is a good deal with a limit then you must pull out your second loyalty card.
- **Buy the smallest size.** - The cost per unit of the bigger box of cereal may be less than the smaller one but with coupons and sales the smaller box is likely a better deal.
- **Coupon policies change** like the wind. Always check for an updated policy before you go shopping. Often you may have to educate the cashier so be prepared.
- **Coupon Pictures** are often the most expensive item. Disregard the picture and read the words. Often you will find you can get a better deal on a similar item.
- **Unadvertised Sales** are better than the advertised sales. You have to do a walk through. Each week stores have great deals that are not advertised. Having

your coupons with you at all times will ensure you catch a hot deal.
- **Be Nice to Everyone** Don't get upset with the cashier and or manager.  Apologize to the person behind you if you are taking to long.  Friendly people make shopping pleasant for everyone.  Angry people steal joy, don't sweat the small stuff.  Keep a smile on your face.
- **Never shop while hungry**

**Don't get couponitis, that's when you go a little coupon crazy and buy things that are dirt cheap in large quantities.  You must remember the manufacturer is not losing;**

**EXAMPLES: if the Jell-o packs go on sale from 2.50 to 2.00 and with your coupon you can get it for 1.00, the manufacturer is still making money.   The cost was only 30 cent, maximum to produce.  You can make Jell-o yourself for .15 homemade.**

**If cake mix is regular 1.79 and goes on sale for 1.25 with your coupon you can get if for .75 cent, remember if you buy the flour, baking soda, etc. it would only cost you maybe .25 to make it yourself from scratch.**

**If the razors go on sale from 10 dollars, for 5 bucks, think how much materials it actually cost to produce.  Maybe about a dollar or so, maximum, so 5 bucks is still too much to pay.**

**So, think before you buy stuff, sometimes what looks like a good deal is not.  The stores aren't losing they get .08 cent plus the value of every coupon they turn in.  The manufacturer is getting his product out, but you can bet they are making money and not giving you stuff at their expense.  So, you be smart on how and where you spend your dollars.**

# DECODING THE BARCODE

Decoding a coupon is necessary to understand how to make the most of it. There is a lot to understand about reading the UPC and GS1 bar code. For this pocket guide I suggest you the quickest way to decode what the coupon is saying is get a free application on your smart phone to do the work for you.

**QSeer**. This app is for iPhones and iPads has one of the most co-founders who have years worth of coupon industry experience. QSeer reads your coupons' bar codes, and tells you how the coupons will scan at the store.

**SnipSnap.** This app is ideal for extreme couponers. You snap a picture of coupons with your smartphone. The app not only captures the coupon, but it also stores the expiration date and provides in-store reminders. It's social, too. You can connect with friends to share coupons.

There are several different applications for Android and Windows phones. Download the free ones and try them out. The couponing applications on your smart phone will help you in saving time, organizing and saving money.

If you like to go more in to detail in please refer to the regular edition.

# 2

# YOUR
# GAME
# PLAN

# Couponing Plans

The quick and easy plan does not take a lot of time or effort. You simply are looking out for the items you need and/or concentrating on one store. This will not deviate you from what you are normally doing. It's fairly simple and not complicated.

# Quick & Easy Plan

- **Make a list of the most used items in your household** – Concentrate on these items only
- **Order Coupons for your Hot Items** – If there is a coupon IT IS GOING TO GO ON SALE!!
- **Get the Newspaper weekly** – check sales paper weekly and look for those items.
- **Organize Coupons** – Place your coupons in a wallet and keep on you at all times.
- **Check weekly for unadvertised sales** – Match sales with coupons and shop like you normally do. Keeping your eye out for when your items goes on sale. **OFTEN THE LOWEST PRICE IS NEVER IN THE SAME WEEK WHEN THE COUPON COMES OUT.** Use patience and don't be in a rush to buy it at the first advertised sale. The item will be listed week after week until it expires.
- **Buy** – When you find the lowest price, buy 6 of the item and begin your stock pile
- **Always check the clearance section!**
- **ONLY USE YOUR COUPON WHEN ITEM IS ON SALE!!**

Go to one store, at the same time every week. Get to know the manager and the cashiers who work that shift. Be friendly. Week after week you will see they will work with you maximize your savings. You will find out about hot deals and you will see the difference. Look out for the cashier and give them extra coupons when you have them. They are your partner in savings!

Don't be so serious, enjoy your trip. Make sure your cashier is enjoying your visit as well. Kill dead time with pleasant conversation. When you come people need to be happy, not upset, cashiers need to welcome you to their lines.

As you concentrate on getting your items, make sure you take advantage of extra deals that you may see. If you don't need the items tell your cashiers, family and friends. Share your knowledge and you will see people will share knowledge with you.

## YOU MUST REMEMBER TO.........

**Watch the cashier**. When checking out pay close attention to the prices to make sure everything is correct. Make sure that all of your coupons scan properly. Coupons sometimes stick together and the cashier does not pay attention. It's your job to check for errors, not theirs. Some store can print out a pre-receipt, check to make sure your totals match.

.

# GATHERING COUPONS

If you get an item for free yahoo, good for you. But why not get 5 for free and save the rest. Chances are the item will not hit that rock bottom price for another six months. So get enough to last you. This is the real value in couponing, but you will need more than one coupon.

- **The Sunday newspaper** is a best source of coupons. Buy the newspaper with the largest circulation in order to get the best coupons. If you are blessed enough your newspaper will offer a double pack.
- **The Internet**. There are many online printable coupons sites.

    ### FINDING COUPONS ONLINE

    http://www.couponnetwork.com/

    http://coupons.com/

    http://redplum.com/

    http://smartsource.com/

    http://couponsuzy.com/

# A COUPLE COUPONING CLIPPING SERVICES

**4 U 2 Coupon**: Located in Illinois (IL). Sells clipped coupons. To order please visit 4U2Coupon.com

**Coupon Beat**: Located in Tennessee (TN). Sells clipped coupons, whole inserts, store coupons and gift cards. To order please visit CouponBeat.com

**Coupons & Things By Dede**: Located in Texas (TX). Sells clipped coupons & whole inserts. To order please visit CouponsThingsByDede.com

**My Coupon Hunter**: Located in Florida (FL). Sells clipped coupons, non-Sunday coupons & gift certificates. To order please visit MyCouponHunter.com

**Rebecca's Coupons & Forms**: Located in Florida (FL). Sells clipped coupons, mail in rebate and other forms & gift certificates. To order please visit CouponsAndForms.com

**The Coupon Clippers**: Located in Florida (FL). Sells clipped coupons, non-Sunday insert coupons, coupon books & coupon organizers. To order please visit TheCouponClippers.com

**The Coupon Master**: Located in Rhode Island (RI). Sells clipped coupons, coupon organizers, shopping list pads & gift certificates. To order please visit TheCouponMaster.com

# STOCK PILE

### What is a Stockpile?

A stock pile is a stock of items that you use for your family. A stockpile is built one item at a time. Set aside a part of your budget for stockpiling. Week by week buy items that are free or unbelievably low and sooner or later you will amass a huge stock. Don't rush this process.

Buy for the future use. If an item goes on sale for a great price (free) then buy more. Typically sales hit the lowest price in 6 months increments. So buy enough for months or if it's something that does not spoil (paper towels, diapers, etc.), maybe a year.

Do your homework now. Start paying attention to how many bottles of body wash, toothpaste, packs of diapers, dish detergent, etc. you use within a time period. This will help you to have a better idea of how much you should buy to begin your stock pile.  Once you have this knowledge you can begin to make your plan.

# REMEMBER

# ROME WAS NOT BUILT IN A DAY,

# NEITHER WILL YOUR STOCK PILE !

KEEP WHAT YOU NEED FOR YOUR FAMILY!!

## DONATE THE REST

Donate if there is no way you will use it before it expires, or you have too much. I personally like to donate to orphanages, you can find one local to your area by searching online at:
Within USA - http://www.missionfinder.org/orphanages.htm
International – http://www.orphanage.com/

My favorite charity is:
JOY RANCH Childrens Home
813 Joy Ranch Road
Woodlawn, VA 24381-1305
(276) 236-5578

Always consider shelters and/or food pantry that will always be grateful for your help.

# 3

# ADDITIONAL
# INFORMATION

# RESOURCES

## EXPIRED COUPONS?

Send them to our troops. The military families can use expired coupons for up to six months. What a great way to support our troops.

**Eligible Coupons:**
Send only Manufacturer **Coupons**
Coupons must be Clipped and Sorted into Food and Non-food (explained below). Do NOT send **coupons** that are over 90 days **expired**.

**Separate your clipped coupons into two categories: Food and Non-Food**
Most military bases have 2 stores. One is called the "Commissary" which is a grocery store and the other is the PX or BX which is a department store. Sort the **coupons** into "food" and "non-food" bundles so that they can be correctly routed once they arrive at the base.

**Germany Ramstein Air Base**
**Attn: Family Services**
**Bldg. 1200**
**APO AE 09094**

**Guam Airman and Family Readiness Center**
**36 MSS/DPF**
**Unit 14001, Box 17**
**APO AP 96543**

**Japan Airman and Family Readiness Center**
**Unit 5134 Box 80**
**18 FSS/FSFR**
**APO AP 96368-5134**

**Japan Airman Kadena Commissary**
**DECA/WP/KAD**
**Unit 5156  Bldg. 407**
**APO  AP 96367-5000**

**Japan Westpac Region**
**Camp Courtney Commissary**
**Unit 5156**
**APO AP 96368-5000**

Japan Yokota Military Couponers
PSC 78 Box 7022
APO AP 96326

Germany USAG Bamberg
IMEU-BAM-MWR-ACS
Army Emergency Relief Manager
CMR 459
APO AE 09139

Germany Grafenwoeher Coupon Coordinator
CMR Box 415 Box 6989
APO AE 09114

Germany Hohenfels Coupon Coordinator
CMR 414 box # 1177
APO, AE 09173

Germany Illesheim Army Community Service
CMR 416
Bldg. 6510
APO AE 09140

Italy Vicenza Army Community Service
US Army Garrison Vicenza
Unit 31401, Box 80
APO AE 09630

UK Lakenheath Airman and Family Readiness Center
48 FSS/FSFR Bldg 950
Unit 5200, Box 105
APO AE 09461

Cuba US NAVY MA3 Wilson
PSC 1005 Box 60
FPO AE 09593

Guam US NAVY Fleet and Family Support Center
Naval Base Guam, Building 106
PSC 455 Box 157
FPO AP 96540

Japan Sasebo US Fleet Activities
Fleet & Family Support Center

**PSC 476 Box 62**
**FPO AP 96322-0062**

I've found the best sites for alternating addresses to our different bases.

The Overseas Coupon Program  http://www.ocpnet.org/ will help you in selecting a site to adopt.

The staff at
**http://www.grocerysavingtips.com/expiredgrocerycoupons.htm** has worked diligently in keeping the addresses updated.

Before you send your coupons please visit either site to make sure that the address is still valid.  They also have a downloadable form letter to include with your coupons and some wonderful thank you notes from our troops☺

If you seek you shall find, search the internet for sites that are particular to your area.  Everything is out there, you will be surprised.  Here are some of my favorites.

## TO FIND OUT SALE BEFORE THE WEEK STARTS

> http://www.totallytarget.com/ - Target

> http://iheartthemart.com – WalMart

> http://iheartpublix.com – Publix

> http://iheartkroger.com - Kroger

## TO FIND IF THERE IS A COUPON FOR A PARTICULAR ITEM

> http://coupontom.com/

# ALSO CHECK OUT EBAY AND OTHER ONLINE AUCTION SITES.

# COUPON TERMINOLOGY

**$1/3 =** A coupon that read one dollar for three items.

**3/$5 =** A coupon that means 3 items for five dollars.

**BLINKIES =** In-store coupons near product, usually from a red blinking box.

**BOGO or B1G1F or B1G1 Free =** Buy One Get One Free.

**CAT or CATALINA =** Coupon that prints at the register after purchase.

**CRT =** Cash register tape, coupon that prints in store.

**DND =** Means Do Not Double – will not double even if store offers doubling.          **DOUBLE COUPON =** Coupon that a grocery store doubles in value.

**ECB =** CVS Extra Care Bucks earned for purchases.

**FREE ITEM COUPON =** A coupon that allows you to get the product completely free.

**GM =** General Mills Coupon

**IVC =** Walgreen's Instant Value Coupon

**IP =** Internet Printable Coupon.

**MFG =** Manufacturer's Coupon.

**MM =** Money Maker

**MIR =** Mail In Rebate.

**NED =** No expiration date.

**OOP =** Out of Pocket, in reference to how much "real money" you will pay at the register.

**OYNO =** On your next order.

**P&G =** Proctor & Gamble Coupon Insert found in the Sunday newspaper.

**PEELIE =** Coupon that you peel off the package.

**PSA =** Prices Starting At.

**Q =** Coupon.

**RP =** Red Plum Coupon Insert found in the Sunday newspaper.

**RR =** Register Rewards.

**SS =** Smart Source coupon insert found in the Sunday newspaper.

**SKIP SKIMMING =** Using a coupon for something it was not intended for.

**STACKING =** Using a store specific coupon with a manufacturer coupon (most stores allow this).

**TEARPAD** = A pad of refund forms or coupons found hanging from a store shelf or display.

**TRIPLE COUPON** = A coupon that a grocery store triples in value.

**WSL** = While Supplies Last

**WYB** = When You Buy.

**YMMV** = Your Mileage May Vary (success of the attempt may vary at your store).

Email the authors to find out about lectures, upcoming events and coupon classes.
Save@couponadvice.info

I trust you will stretch your dollars and maximize your shopping experiences. Find the joy in mastering the markets. The stores are working hard on trying to trick you out your money, now go work hard on how to save it.

# Go get em' Grasshopper!!

www.ingramcontent.com/pod-product-compliance
Lightning Source LLC
Chambersburg PA
CBHW040317010626
45792CB00022B/692